Tree to Paper

by Rachel Grack

BLASTOFF!
2
READERS

BELLWETHER MEDIA • MINNEAPOLIS, MN

Note to Librarians, Teachers, and Parents:

Blastoff! Readers are carefully developed by literacy experts and combine standards-based content with developmentally appropriate text.

Level 1 provides the most support through repetition of high-frequency words, light text, predictable sentence patterns, and strong visual support.

Level 2 offers early readers a bit more challenge through varied simple sentences, increased text load, and less repetition of high-frequency words.

Level 3 advances early-fluent readers toward fluency through increased text and concept load, less reliance on visuals, longer sentences, and more literary language.

Level 4 builds reading stamina by providing more text per page, increased use of punctuation, greater variation in sentence patterns, and increasingly challenging vocabulary.

Level 5 encourages children to move from "learning to read" to "reading to learn" by providing even more text, varied writing styles, and less familiar topics.

Whichever book is right for your reader, Blastoff! Readers are the perfect books to build confidence and encourage a love of reading that will last a lifetime!

This edition first published in 2020 by Bellwether Media, Inc.

No part of this publication may be reproduced in whole or in part without written permission of the publisher. For information regarding permission, write to Bellwether Media, Inc., Attention: Permissions Department, 6012 Blue Circle Drive, Minnetonka, MN 55343.

Library of Congress Cataloging-in-Publication Data

LC record for Tree to Paper available at https://lccn.loc.gov/2019026825

Text copyright © 2020 by Bellwether Media, Inc. BLASTOFF! READERS and associated logos are trademarks and/or registered trademarks of Bellwether Media, Inc.

Editor: Rebecca Sabelko   Designer: Laura Sowers

Printed in the United States of America, North Mankato, MN.

Table of Contents

Paper Beginnings

Did you know paper
is made from trees?

Where Is Paper Made?

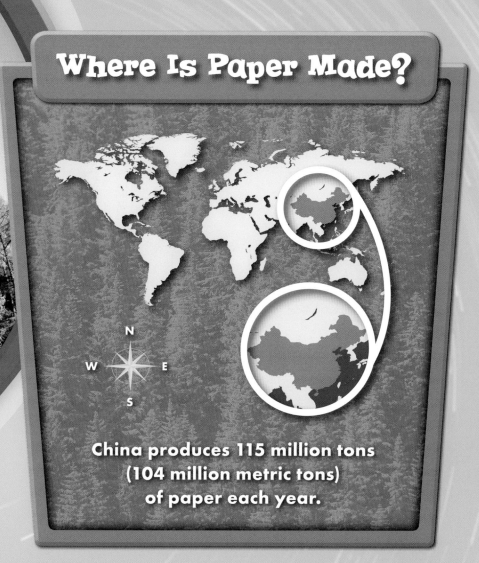

China produces 115 million tons
(104 million metric tons)
of paper each year.

Forest plantations are home to fast-growing trees. The trees are **processed** into the paper we use every day!

Forest to Mill

After a few years of growth,
trees are ready to **harvest**.
Loggers cut them down and
remove the branches.

What Makes a Tree Grow?

soil

water

sunlight

Trucks are loaded with logs.
They head to paper mills!

spinning drum

At the mill, the logs go through a spinning drum. This removes the bark.

The logs then get chopped up in the **chipper**.

Wood chips are cooked with **chemicals** to break down **lignin**.

The chips turn into a brown, watery **pulp**. The pulp is cleaned and whitened.

pulp

Recycled Paper

1 out of every 3 paper goods is made from recycled paper

paper mill

wood chips

Making Paper

The pulp is sprayed
onto a moving screen.
As water drains out, **fibers**
in the pulp join together.

They form a long, solid sheet of paper.

paper machine

The wet paper goes through
a paper machine.

Rollers flatten it and press out water. Then heated rollers finish drying the paper.

heavy rollers

One last set of heavy rollers smooths the paper.

The long sheet winds onto a huge **reel**. This gets cut into smaller rolls.

reel

Machines cut rolls of paper into sheets. They get stacked, wrapped, and shipped to stores!

Tree to Paper

1 trees are harvested and taken to mills

2 logs are chopped into wood chips

3 pulp is sprayed onto screens and formed into paper

4 paper is wound onto reels and cut into sheets

5 paper is wrapped and shipped to stores

Trees become all sorts
of paper goods.

Drawing paper is
a favorite. It holds the
pictures you make!

Glossary

chemicals—substances that form when two or more other substances come together

chipper—a machine that chops logs into wood chips

fibers—strings of wood

forest plantations—large tree farms

harvest—to gather crops

lignin—the glue-like material that holds wood together

processed—prepared through a number of steps

pulp—soft, wet wood chips that have been broken down

reel—a spool

To Learn More

AT THE LIBRARY

Best, B.J. *Wood to Paper.* New York, N.Y.: Cavendish Square, 2017.

Meister, Cari. *From Trees to Paper.* Mankato, Minn.: Amicus Ink, 2020.

Sohn, Emily, and Pamela Wright. *Paper from Wood.* Chicago, Ill.: Norwood House Press, 2019.

ON THE WEB

FACTSURFER

Factsurfer.com gives you a safe, fun way to find more information.

1. Go to www.factsurfer.com.

2. Enter "tree to paper" into the search box and click $\mathcal{Q}$.

3. Select your book cover to see a list of related web sites.

Index